J+   Bredeson, Carmen
594.147   Can you find
Bre   these seashells?
ezr $15.95

Can You Find These Seashells?

Carmen Bredeson and Lindsey Cousins

Enslow Elementary
an imprint of
Enslow Publishers, Inc.
40 Industrial Road
Box 398
Berkeley Heights, NJ 07922
USA
http://www.enslow.com

Enslow Elementary, an imprint of Enslow Publishers, Inc.
Enslow Elementary® is a registered trademark of Enslow Publishers, Inc.

Library of Congress Cataloging-in-Publication Data

Bredeson, Carmen.
   Can you find these seashells? / Carmen Bredeson and Lindsey Cousins.
      p. cm. — (All about nature)
   Includes index.
   Summary: "Introduces pre-readers to simple concepts about seashells using short sentences
and repetition of words"—Provided by publisher.
   ISBN 978-0-7660-3978-0
   1. Shells—Juvenile literature. I. Cousins, Lindsey. II. Title.
   QL405.2.B68 2012
   594.147'7—dc23
                                          2011031132
Future editions:
Paperback ISBN 978-1-4644-0068-1
ePUB ISBN 978-1-4645-0975-9
PDF ISBN 978-1-4646-0975-6

Printed in China
012012 Leo Paper Group, Heshan City, Guangdong, China
10 9 8 7 6 5 4 3 2 1

To Our Readers: We have done our best to make sure all Internet Addresses in this book
were active and appropriate when we went to press. However, the author and the publisher
have no control over and assume no liability for the material available on those Internet sites
or on other Web sites they may link to. Any comments or suggestions can be sent by e-mail
to comments@enslow.com or to the address on the back cover.

Photo Credits: © 2011 Photos.com, a division of Getty Images. All rights reserved., pp. 1, 4,
12, 13; Shutterstock.com, pp. 3, 6, 8, 14, 18, 20, 22, 23; Jane Katirgis, pp. 10, 16.

Cover Photo: © 2011 Photos.com, a division of Getty Images. All rights reserved.

Note to Parents and Teachers

Help pre-readers get a jump start on reading. These lively stories introduce simple concepts
with repetition of words and short simple sentences. Photos and illustrations fill the pages
with color and effectively enhance the text. Free Educator Guides are available for this
series at www.enslow.com. Search for the *All About Nature* series name.

Contents

Words to Know

grooves
(groovz)

lightning
(LYT ning)

3

Seashells

Seashells are homes.

Soft little animals live inside.

The hard shells keep them safe.

Look out for shells with

animals in them.

Don't touch them.

You can pick up empty seashells.

Can you find some of the seashells

in this book?

wings

Scallops

Scallop shells are shaped

like fans.

They are many colors.

Scallop shells are many sizes.

Look at the smallest part

of the shell.

Little pieces stick out.

They look like wings.

Do you see the wings?

Coquinas

Coquinas live in sand

near the ocean.

Ocean waves move over the shells.

Tiny bits of food are in the ocean.

Coquinas eat the bits of food.

Coquina shells are small.

Sometimes the shells open up.

Don't you think they look

like butterflies?

An animal
lived in here.

Slippers

Slipper shells look like tiny shoes.

Look at the inside of a slipper shell.

There is a little hole.

An animal lived in there.

A slipper shell is light.

Put one in the water on its back.

It will float.

Conchs

Conch shells can grow very big.

They can be heavy too.

Put your ear next to the opening.

Some people hear the ocean.

Do you hear the ocean too?

Clams

There are many kinds of clams.

Some clams are round.

Some are long and thin.

Some clam shells are big.

Some are small.

Have you ever seen a clam shell?

Oysters

Oysters live in big groups

called "beds."

Oyster beds are under water.

Oyster shells are thick and bumpy.

The edges can be sharp.

Be careful when you pick one up.

Cockles

Cockle shells are white or tan.

The outside has many *grooves*.

The inside is shiny.

Cockle shells can open up.

They look like little bowls.

Find a cockle shell on the beach.

Use it as a shovel.

Lightning Whelks

Lightning whelk shells are

wide on one end.

The other end is pointy.

The inside is smooth.

There are lines on the outside.

The lines look like flashes

of lightning.

That is how the shell got its name.

Mussels

Mussels live in big piles.

They get food from the water.

Some mussels are dark blue.

Others are black.

Mussel shells are smooth on the outside.

Look for a pile of mussels on the beach.

Read More

Cumberbatch, Judy. *Can You Hear the Sea?* New York: Bloomsbury Children's Books, 2007.

Squire, Ann. *Seashells*. New York: Children's Press, 2002.

Wallace, Nancy. *Shells! Shells! Shells!* Tarrytown, N.Y.: Marshall Cavendish, 2007.

Web Sites

Monterey Bay Aquarium <http://www.montereybayaquarium.org/lc/activities/coloring_pages.asp>

Enchanted Learning. *The Beach.* <http://www.enchantedlearning.com/themes/beach.shtml>

Index

Guided Reading Level: E
Guided Reading Leveling System is based on the guidelines recommended by Fountas and Pinnell.

Word Count: 365